COLOURING BOOK
JAPANESE ART
KATSUSHIKA HOKUSAI

Contents

Colouring pencils at the ready!

Originally known as "painting books", colouring books first came into being in the 18th century, the brainchild of various painters and educationists who felt the need to promote the practice of art among young people. This enjoyable pastime, recognized as improving the cognitive ability of those who engage in it, went hand in hand with the arrival of colouring pencils and became popular at the end of the 19th century with the appearance of the first colouring books. These were originally marketed by New York publishers McLoughlin in 1879 and became commonly used by children in the early 1930s. Colouring is an activity accessible to all, both male and female. It is a fascinating and relaxing pastime that helps to promote good motor skills and to develop concentration. Just one key quality is needed: patience. If this is something you lack at times, engaging in this very calming activity is bound to be of benefit. Whether or not you choose to follow the advice we give you here is up to you. The important thing is to let one single objective guide the way you colour: unbridled enjoyment.

Getting started

To feel relaxed when colouring, it's a good idea to create your own space. Gather together everything you need so that you can enjoy your colouring without interruption.

USING PAINTS

BRUSHES

Arm yourself with a selection of brushes of different shapes and thicknesses. Go for quality: nothing is more annoying that a brush that loses its bristles!

PAINTS

Gouache is a very easy medium to use. Soluble and washable in water, it gives bright, intense tones, even when heavily diluted. The colours also blend easily.

In principle, you only really need red, blue, and yellow. With these primary colours, plus a tube of white and one of black, you can create all other colours.

It's up to you to decide how much time you want to spend mixing them!

APPLICATION

Mix your colours on a palette. Make enough to cover all the areas you'll want to paint, as it can be difficult to mix exactly the same tone again. Depending on the intensity you want, add more or less water.

Don't overload your brush with paint, and keep a light hand. If the colour isn't intense enough, go back over it, keeping a light touch. You'll soon find out how to adapt what you do to obtain the desired result. And there's nothing to stop you varying thicknesses within the same area.

USING PENCILS

COLOURING PENCILS

When choosing colouring pencils, go for "artist quality" rather than children's pencils. Good quality pencils are softer and less dry, making it easier to blend the colours and achieve more sustained or subtle tones. Before buying an entire set, try different pencils out; this will help you decide which brand you prefer. Keep them in a small plastic container within easy reach, but make sure it's stored in a safe place to prevent the pencils from breaking.

SHARPENERS

If possible, choose a mechanical sharpener that lets you sharpen pencils of different sizes and protects the coloured lead. Failing this, go for a good quality, manual, metal sharpener which can also be useful for sharpening very short pencils. Don't press too hard when you sharpen, as you could break the lead.

ERASERS

Make sure you have vinyl erasers in different sizes so that, if necessary, you can erase very small details, or small areas of colour. You can also use them to lighten colours. But be careful not to press too hard or you may damage the paper.

APPLICATION

Begin by checking that your pencils are finely sharpened: this will ensure they give the best, most even results.

You can apply colour in several layers until you obtain the colour density you want. Try one or two very light layers, then gradually increase the pressure, which should remain constant throughout the layer.

If you want to blend colours, alternate the layers. Starting with one or two common background layers, apply different colours to different areas to create a range of shades – if you want to add tone to the sky, for example.

By applying colour in small, overlapping circles, you'll avoid hard lines that can be difficult to soften. Try to work consistently, keeping the same movement and the same pressure.

DON'T FORGET

• A good, stable water pot for cleaning your brushes and diluting your paint. Change the water frequently.

• A rag to wipe your brushes or pencil leads after sharpening ... and your fingers!

• A ruler, which is useful as a guide.

• Paper tissues to absorb any surplus paint and soften pencil lines.

Katsushika Hokusai

1760-1849

A spectacular destiny

Hokusai was the most prolific artist of his day. He had a long life (1760-1849) that certainly contributed to his enormous productivity – over 30,000 works are now attributed to him. Moreover, Hokusai's work was extremely diverse, and bears witness to his great skill in all types of painting and drawing. He was a craftsman working in ukiyo-e, which literally means "pictures of the floating world" but referred to a particular school of painting and graphic art. Ukiyo-e gave Hokusai the bedrock for his subsequent mastery of a wide variety of disciplines, from printing (both one-off pictures and series) to book engraving, from traditional genres to epic paintings. His lifestyle was modest, however, and throughout his career he subsisted by balancing his drawing and printmaking with more sporadic ventures into writing and illustrating popular stories, all under a variety of names: Shunro, Hokusai, Taito, Tatsumasa, Gakyojin Hokusai, Hokusai Katsushika, Zen Hokusai Iitsi, Manji, and many more.

Hokusai was born in 1760 in a district of Edo (which came to be known as Tokyo in 1868). He was adopted at the age of three by a craftsman who made mirrors for the court of the Shogun, and he quickly showed a great aptitude for drawing. From the age of 13 he began to serve as an apprentice for various artisans and printers, and a spell as an assistant to a famous Edo bookseller sparked a passion for books. When Hokusai turned 18, he decided to make painting into his career and began to work under the master Shunsho in an ukiyo-e printing studio specializing in portraits of actors. Hokusai's exceptional talent was immediately recognized, but the death of his master precipitated his expulsion from the studio by Shunsho's chief disciple. This setback seems to have triggered some kind of identity crisis, which was compounded by a plunge into dire poverty. To escape this desperate situation, Hokusai started to branch out into a whole range of graphic styles.

Around this time, Hokusai met a fellow artist called Shiba Kokan, who had made friends with the Dutch crew of the only ship authorized to dock, once a year, in Nagasaki. (Since the 1630s Japan had been closed to the outside world, under pain of death, as a protection against proselytization by the Jesuits, who were considered religious colonizers.) The captain of the Dutch ship is said to have paid Hokusai a generous price, strictly under the counter, for a series of prints. Shiba Kokan also initiated Hokusai into the principles of Western perspective and encouraged him to sign his work in European style.

The first steps

In 1795, Hokusai became part of a new school of classical art, which would bring him success through his illustrations of poetry. Around a year later he had obtained a host of commissions, and a degree of fame, for surimonos, prints on simple sheets of paper, designed for private use and serving a function similar to that of greeting cards or invitation slips.

After a while Hokusai turned to painting to broaden his artistic skills. In 1804 he created a spectacular masterpiece by using a broom, soaked in bucketfuls of Indian ink, to paint a gigantic portrait in the courtyard of a temple in Edo. It depicted a Daruma (a seminal figure in Buddhist history, always shown with a bald head, large round eyes and profuse beard) on a canvas covering nearly 2,700 sq. ft, hung from the roof down to the floor for all to see. He would go on to repeat this performance in 1817, this time in Nagoya.

At the age of 40 Hokusai declared himself to be "mad about art". He was determined to depart from hackneyed subject matter by immersing himself in all the sights offered by the streets of Edo, which he hardly ever left. His work drew inspiration from simple folk and their daily activities and shared concerns. Nagoya in 1814 proved life-changing, as it led to an encounter with another artist called Bokusen and the subsequent publication of Hokusai's Manga (sketches). Bokusen and his colleagues were immediately bowled over by the originality, humour and daring of Hokusai's innumerable sketchbooks. In this array of drawings, studies and caricatures assembled in picture books and printed in black with pink and grey highlights, Hokusai captured everyday scenes without any prejudice or inhibition. He broke down and simplified the movements of wrestlers and acrobats, the delicate gestures of dancers and jugglers and the mannerisms of ordinary people, whether old or young, fat or thin. These prints met with considerable success over the course of twenty years. Hokusai also occasionally branched out into more specific subjects, such as architecture and landscape.

When Hokusai turned 60 he suddenly adopted the name Iitsu, which means "age of an extra year", and threw himself into illustrating books. In 1827 he recovered from a stroke, without any outside assistance, but shortly afterwards in the summer of that year, his wife died. From then on his sole companion would be his daughter Oyei, an artist in her own right, who would give him much-appreciated support until the end of his life.

Hokusai's masterpiece

The year 1831 saw the appearance of a series of Thirty-Six Views of Mount Fuji that would earn Hokusai worldwide recognition. Each print recorded a view of the famous volcano from a different vantage point. This series also featured Hokusai's first use of Prussian Blue, which had arrived in Japan in 1829, and this new element gave his work a highly distinctive tone and look. These prints reflect the aesthetic principles outlined in Hokusai's preface to his Quick Lessons in Simplified Drawing: "Every form has its own dimensions, which we must respect, but we must not forget that these things belong to a universe whose harmony we must never shatter. My art of painting is like this". The runaway success of Thirty-Six Views of Mount Fuji led to other extremely popular series on a range of subjects: waterfalls, bridges, birds and ghosts (the latter was cut short after only five prints).

Hokusai's great productivity and eclecticism can be attributed to his absolute mastery of every stage of the technical process of woodblock printing, which he had acquired during his apprenticeship in specialist studios. The first step consisted of an initial drawing with simple strokes of black Indian ink on translucent paper. This drawing was then entrusted to an engraver, who put the sheet of paper upside down on a cherry-wood block so that he could carve out the lines of the drawing with chisels and knives, reproducing their upstrokes and downstrokes, their thickness and their opacity. The contours of the drawing therefore emerged in relief, and this first block was used to make a print with black ink. On the basis of this monochrome test, the artist decided on the different layers of colour that would make up the final print, and the engraver would then set about carving out a new block for each colour. These blocks were then passed on to the printer, who played a vital role in the process (described by Hokusai as "cooking the drawings") as he was responsible for carefully balancing the various shades of colour, in accordance with the artist's instructions, in order to achieve subtleties of light and shade.

Drawing and wisdom

In 1834, shortly after the publication of a further series of One Hundred Views of Mount Fuji, Hokusai left Edo, to escape the repercussions of the irresponsible behaviour of a young man from his family. He stayed in Suruga, on the Miura peninsula, and while he was there he started publishing his last major series: illustrations of traditional poems, under the title One Hundred Poems by One Hundred Poets Explained by the Wet Nurse. Hokusai only returned to Edo in 1836, the year of the Great Famine, which he survived by trading some of his artworks for rice. These precarious conditions forced him to give up One Hundred Poems after completing only 27 prints.

In 1839, a fire in Hokusai's studio destroyed all the drawings that he had in storage. After this disaster, he drastically reduced his output, which until then had been frenetic. Over the last ten years of his life he produced less and less, although every morning he set about drawing a karashishi, a legendary sacred lion endowed with supernatural powers. This exercise, which was more of a ritual or prayer, involved a ceaseless exploration of the same subject, the same form and the same line. The resulting 219 drawings were assembled in a single book, prefaced by Hokusai's observation: "Every morning I started drawing, in the hope of a peaceful day". In 1845 he embarked on one final journey, to visit a friend in Shinano province, and while he was there he painted his last pictures, inside a temple.

Hokusai died in the spring of 1849. Legend has it that his last words on his deathbed were: "Five more years and I would have become a great artist". His ashes were buried in a cemetery near the Keikyoji temple, in the neighbourhood where he had spent much of his life. His tomb bears the following epitaph: "Oh freedom, beautiful freedom, when one leaves to walk towards the summer fields, a soul alone, far from the body!"

A highly influential artist

Unfortunately, Hokusai was largely forgotten soon after his death, but two factors led to a subsequent reassessment of his exceptional talent. Firstly, Japan's opening-up to the outside world and, secondly, the interest of the Impressionists (and, gradually, the whole of Europe) in Japanese art. Monet was one of the first painters to become fascinated by Japanese prints and their influence can be seen in many of his paintings.

Long before his last breath, "art-mad" Hokusai, in his all-embracing quest to bear witness to the world around him, fulfilled his dream of bringing to life the tiniest dot and the subtlest line: "At the age of six I started to draw all kinds of things. By the age of fifty I had already drawn a lot, but nothing that I did before my seventieth year was worthy of mention. It was only at the age of seventy-three that I started to understand the true form of animals, insects and fish, and the nature of plants and trees. Consequently, by the age of eighty-six I will have made more and more progress and, at ninety I will have penetrated still further the essence of art. At one hundred, I will have definitely achieved a wonderful level, and at one hundred and ten every dot and every line in my drawings will have its own life. I would like to ask those who outlive me to certify that I have not been mistaken".

Taro Moon
1797-1798, woodblock print.
22.7 × 16.5 cm.

Noh theatre is a Japanese classical genre combining poetry with dance and mime. It was basically performed for shogun (military chiefs) and samurai (warriors), with all the parts being played by men. The costumes and in particular the masks (smaller than the face and designed to evoke all kinds of emotions) exhibit special features that convey precise information about the type of character being portrayed. The two actors depicted here are taking part in a *kyogen*, a comic interlude performed between two *Noh* pieces. The main actor wears a magnificent and voluminous kimono that flows under a large parasol held by a servant (recognizable as such by the fact that he does not wear a mask).

Taro Moon, 1797-1798.

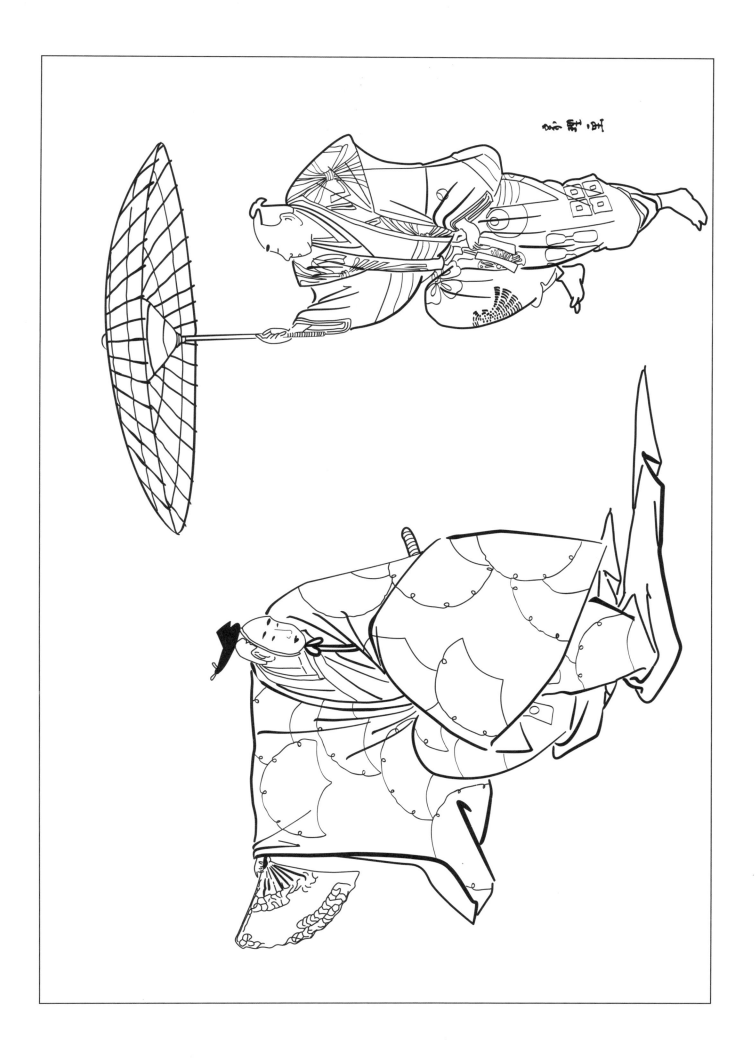

Taro Moon, 1797-1798.

Act 1 (Shodan)

Taken from the series *The Treasury of Loyal Retainers*.
C. 1798, woodblock print.
25.1 × 37 cm.

This print illustrates one of the most famous popular stories of the Edo period, *The Revenge of the 47 Ronin* or *Chushingura*, which explores the theme of loyalty to masters. Like many artists before him, Hokusai revelled in this subject's wealth of characters and picturesque scenes. Here, a wife is shown standing in the centre of the print, between her servant (left), and a suitor whose advances she rejects. Her back is arched, in a highly stylized pose that emphasizes her indignation and outrage. This rigid posture is reminiscent of the way Japanese theatre actors often freeze momentarily in position to draw attention to particularly important points in their performances.

Act I (Shodan), C. 1798.

Act I (*Shodan*), C. 1798.

Act V (Godanme)

Taken from the series *The Treasury of Loyal Retainers*.
C. 1798, woodblock print.
22 × 32.7 cm.

Kanpei, a faithful servant, vows to avenge the death of his master. He looks for help from his father-in-law, Yoichibei, who agrees to sell his daughter to raise the money needed for this purpose. While travelling together, however, Yoichibei is attacked and killed by a brigand, while Kanpei is busy shooting a wild boar. On returning to the road and finding the dead body, Kanpei believes that he himself has accidentally killed the old man. This moment from Act V of *Chushingura* (a famous Japanese story) depicts the attack on the old man. In the distance the wild boar is shown fleeing to safety, giving the scene an unsettling and poignant twist, as the viewer knows that the unfortunate Kanpei, whose presence here is only suggested, will soon be held responsible for a crime that he has not committed.

Act V (*Godanme*), C. 1798.

Act V (Godanme), C. 1798.

Shirabyoshi Dancer

C 1820, woodblock print.

98 × 41.9 cm.

Shirabyoshi was a dance accompanied by singing that was performed in the royal court by women dressed as men. This style was extremely fashionable from the 12th to the 16th centuries. The songs were slow but rhythmic, and specially designed to accompany the distinctive gestures of the dance. *Shirabyoshi* dancers were frequently summoned to perform in court cermonies attended by samurai. The dancer portrayed here has all the traditional accoutrements of her profession: a white robe, *nagabakama* (ornate red trousers), a ceremonial sword, and a fan. Her pose indicates that she is in the process of introducing the upcoming performance.

This print is signed "Hokusai taito aratame Iitsu hitsu," and stamped with the seal KATSUHIKA, denoting the artist's recent change in style.

Shirabyoshi Dancer, C. 1820.

Shirabyoshi Dancer, C. 1820.

Samurai on Horseback

1826, woodblock print.

31.6 × 45.4 cm.

This watercolour is a mystery. How did Hokusai manage to obtain both the paper and the traditional Dutch crayons needed to carry it out? This equestrian portrait formed part of the collection of a Dutch captain – undoubtedly the same one who, according to legend, secretly bought a large batch of Hokusai's work.

Apart from the colours typical of the *ukiyo-e* ("pictures of the floating world"), there are also touches of indigo and Prussian Blue on the clothes of the samurai, and on the peasants working in the ricefield. The maze of paths stretching towards the horizon shows how quickly Hokusai mastered the principles of perspective and depth of field.

Samurai on Horseback, 1826.

Samurai on Horseback, 1826.

Great Wave Off Kanagawa

Taken from the series *Thirty-Six Views of Mount Fuji*.
C. 1830-1832, woodblock print.
25.9 × 38 cm.

Is there anyone who hasn't seen the *Great Wave*? The world-famous print quickly found success way beyond Japan and had a particularly strong impact on the Impressionists.

Hokusai set about depicting three essential elements in each of the *Thirty-Six Views of Mount Fuji*: the divine, the human, and the earthly. This composition is perfectly balanced: the gigantic wave, like a gaping mouth, threatening to engulf the flimsy boats while their crew members cling to each other in fear, defenceless against this force of nature. In the distance rises Mount Fuji, which could be confused at first sight with the foam on the tips of the waves. Its reassuring immutable presence amidst all this fury offers glimpses of a calm resolution to this violent upheaval.

Great Wave Off Kanagawa, C. 1830-1832.

Great Wave Off Kanagawa, C. 1830-1832.

Mount Fuji on a Clear Day

Taken from the series *Thirty-Six Views of Mount Fuji*.
C. 1830-1832, woodblock print.
38 × 37.8 cm.

This depiction of Mount Fuji, also known as *Red Fuji*, is equally as famous as the previous print. It was painted in the early morning (hence the shimmering hues). The mountain rears up to the right, against a blue background, while at the foot of its rugged slopes small black dots are clustered together to represent a forest.

These sharply contrasting proportions allow the mountain to dominate the landscape. The power of the composition is partly derived not only from the simplicity of its forms but also from the use of only three basic colours: Prussian Blue for the sky (spreading into green for the trees), red for the volcano, and white for the snow and clouds.

Mount Fuji on a Clear Day, C. 1830-1832.

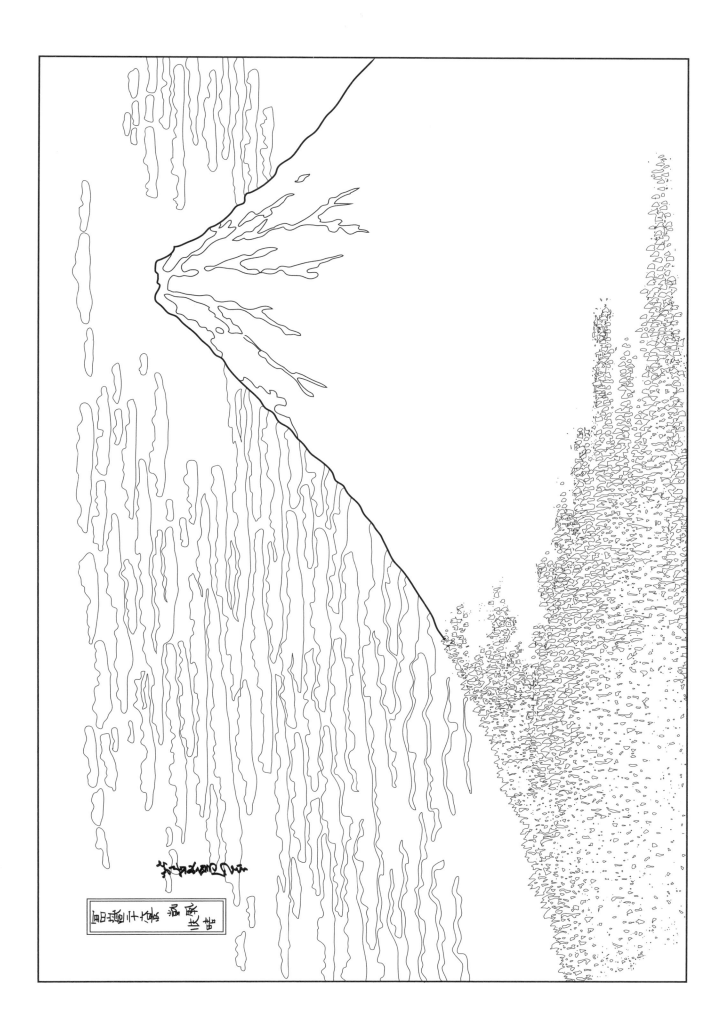

Mount Fuji on a Clear Day, C. 1830-1832.

People Admiring Mount Fuji from a Teahouse in Yoshida

Taken from the series *Thirty-Six Views of Mount Fuji*.
C. 1830-1832, woodblock print.
26 × 38 cm.

The tea ceremony is one of the emblems of Japanese tradition. A teahouse has at least two rooms: one where the tea is prepared, another where it is drunk. The characters in this print are gathered together in the tokonoma (a raised alcove typical of teahouses), admiring the distant Mount Fuji through a large window. The two men to the right of the composition seem to be sleeping while the servant points out the snow-topped volcano to the two women. In the foreground, an emaciated old man is beating a wicker sandal with a hammer to soften it.

Also worthy of note is the striking difference between the near nakedness of the characters to the left, and the heavy clothing of the others.

People Admiring Mount Fuji from a Teahouse in Yoshida,
C. 1830-1832.

People Admiring Mount Fuji from a Teahouse in Yoshida,
C. 1830-1832.

Back View of Mount Fuji from the Minobu River

Taken from the series *Thirty-Six Views of Mount Fuji*.
C. 1830-1832, woodblock print.
25.6 × 37.6 cm.

The outline of the snow-topped volcano is immediately recognizable in this misty landscape, even though the two craggy cliffs in the foreground initially attract our attention. Mount Fuji seems to be watching over the small figures going along the path to the roaring river, and Hokusai uses its symbolic power to create a comforting presence.

Both the two horses and the people on the narrow path – travellers, pilgrims, peasants, and even a sedan chair – seem to be trudging along wearily. The dense textures of the white mass of clouds, which splits the composition into two, endow this print with an air of mystery.

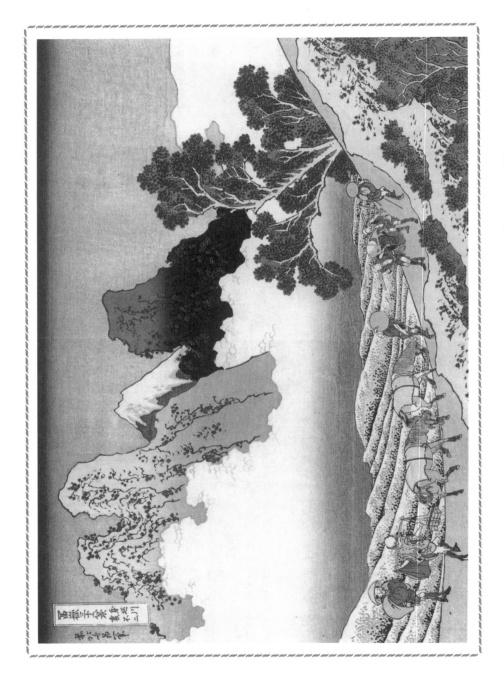

Back View of Mount Fuji From the Minobu River, C. 1830-1832.

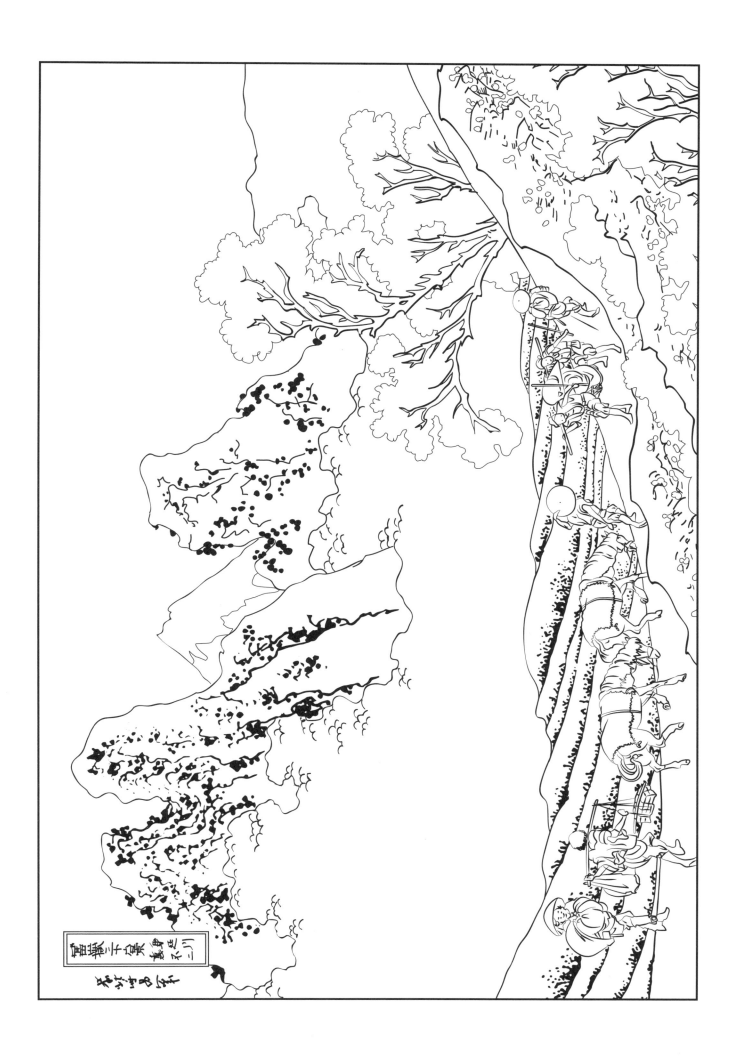

Back View of Mount Fuji From the Minobu River, C. 1830-1832.

Falcon and Cherry Blossoms

Taken from the series *Great Images of Nature*.
1832-1833, woodblock print.
50.2 × 22.2 cm.

The flowering cherry tree is a classic subject in Japanese painting as it is a symbol of ephemeral beauty. The blossoming of the *sakura* (its Japanese name) is also a recurring theme in literature, dancing, theatre and religion. Hokusai, who was undoubtedly familiar with the Japanese proverb "the intelligent falcon hides its talons from its enemy", sets off the delicacy of the flowery branch against the power of this predator. The bird, with its meticulously drawn plumage, is shown against a background of petals, their gleaming whiteness sharply contrasting with the darkness of the feathers. Despite the falcon's strength and threatening nature, Hokusai has made him look slightly stupid, as if wanting to prove the famous maxim wrong.

Falcon and Cherry Blossoms,
1832-1833.

Falcon and Cherry Blossoms,
1832-1833.

Autumn in Choko

Taken from the series *Eight Views of Ryukyu*.
1833, woodblock print.
25.8 × 37.9 cm.

This print evokes autumn (*koyo* in Japanese), which starts on the island of Hokkaido in mid-September and finishes in mid-December in the Tokyo region. Like springtime (*hanami*), koyo gives rise to ancient rituals in which crowds flock to designated spots, including temples, to contemplate the beauty of the colours associated with the changing of the season.

In this print, however, Hokusai presents the opposite of these busy places: an uninhabited landscape, where the only human presence (apart from the people onboard the boats) is two men crossing a bridge. This is extremely long and narrow, further emphasizing the impression of isolation – as do the scattered islets that emerge from the pale blue mist.

Autumn in Choko, 1833.

Autumn in Choko, 1833.

The Chinese Poet Li Bai

Taken from the series *A True Mirror of Chinese and Japanese Poetry*.
1833-1834, woodblock print.

52.1 × 23.2 cm.

Li Bai (c. 700-762), better known as the "immortal poet" and often considered the greatest Chinese poet of all time, is shown here facing the imposing waterfall on Mount Lu in the Kiangsi region. He was famous in his day for using copious alcohol consumption as a stimulus for his imagination, which is undoubtedly why Hokusai chose to depict him propped up by two of his students (even though he is leaning on a staff) as he stands on the edge of a precipice.

Hokusai adroitly conveys the feeling of vertigo induced by this spot through both the unsteady balance of the poet confronting the void, and the slant of the pine tree on the cliff opposite him. The composition is counterbalanced by the impetuous mass of the cascading water.

The Chinese Poet Li Bai,
1833-1834.

The Chinese Poet Li Bai, 1833-1834.

The Chinese Poet Su Dongpo

Taken from the series *A True Mirror of Chinese and Japanese Poetry*.
1833-1834, woodblock print.
42.7 × 22.5 cm.

Su Dongpo (1036-1101) was a mandarin (a high-ranking government official in the Chinese Empire) but also a poet, calligrapher, and painter who celebrated nature throughout his life. It is therefore not surprising that Hokusai shows him here on horseback, seen from the rear as he contemplates the landscape shrouded in snow. Beside him, his servant seems to be questioning him with his gaze. They have stopped on a natural promontory eroded out of the rocks, which dominates the composition, while also appearing to be weightless. Everything is covered by snow, which has erased all the contours of the landscape and blurred the lines between sky and water, foreground and background, high and low.

The Chinese Poet Su Dongpo, 1833-1834.

The Chinese Poet Su Dongpo, 1833-1834.

Noboto in Shimosa Province

Taken from the series *One Thousand Pictures of the Ocean*.
1833-1834, woodblock print.
18.3 × 24.8 cm.

In the series *One Thousand Pictures of the Ocean*, Hokusai explored the different fishing methods used in the various provinces of Japan. The organization of the landscape in this particular print revolves around a division into three distinct sections. In the foreground, some men can be seen gathering shellfish on the shore, each equipped with a basket. Then the sea covers almost the entirety of the picture, its expanse broken only by a solitary boat, while subtle variations in its blue colour suggest the depths lurking beneath. Finally, to the rear, a rolling landscape runs down to the fishermens' huts on the beach, where tiny figures can also be seen foraging for shellfish.

Noboto, in Shimosa Province, 1833-1834.

Noboto, in Shimosa Province, 1833-1834.

Canary and Small Peonies

Taken from the series *Little Flowers*.
1834, woodblock print.
24.3 × 17.9 cm.

In his series *Little Flowers*, Hokusai often put his subjects against a dark blue background to set off the colours of the flowers he was drawing – in this case, orange peonies, which contrast with the yellow of a hovering canary. By isolating the flowers as if they were being seen through a telescope, Hokusai moves our gaze away from the centre in order to heighten the illusion that their petals and stems are being ruffled by a light breeze.

The balance of this composition is masterly: the blue of the sky frames the bunch of flowers and gives it a powerful immediacy, while the canary, in its turn, is surrounded by the peonies. In this series, the inscriptions of the botanical names are written in Chinese characters.

Canary and Small Peonies, 1834.

Canary and Small Peonies, 1834.

Kirifuri Waterfall, on Mount Kurokami, Shimotsuke

Taken from the series *A Tour of the Waterfalls of the Provinces*.
1834-1835, woodblock print.
18.9 × 26.3 cm.

Found to the north of Edo, in the mountainous region of Nikko, the spectacular Kirifuri Waterfall still attracts many visitors today. In his triumphantly successful *Waterfalls* series, Hokusai tackled this subject by using vertical compositions and showing his sightseers having to look upwards to admire the scenery. In this print, Hokusai also seems to be carefully observing the other travellers who have ventured to this spot. The use of blue lines to depict water recalls the techniques that contributed to the success of the Great Wave. It seems that Hokusai loved to play with these lines purely for the sheer pleasure of the composition.

Kirifuri Waterfall, on Mount Kurokami, Shimotsuke,
1834-1835.

Kirifuri Waterfall, on Mount Kurokami, Shimotsuke,
1834-1835.

"The Hanging-Cloud Bridge" on Mount Gyodo, Ashikaga

Taken from the series *Remarkable Views of Bridges in Various Provinces*.
C. 1834, woodblock print.
25.7 × 38.4 cm.

"The Hanging-Cloud Bridge" on Mount Gyodo, Ashikaga was entirely the fruit of Hokusai's imagination, like most of the structures that he drew for the series *Remarkable Views of Bridges in Various Provinces*, which features a wide range of bridges amidst their natural settings. As the view shown here does not actually exist, it has a dreamlike, almost idealized quality.

A small isolated hut, perched on a rock, is connected to the rest of the scene by the delicate thin line of a wooden bridge, which is the central element in the composition. Despite the absence of human beings (unusual in Hokusai's work), it seems clear that the occupant of the hut must be an ascetic who has withdrawn from the world.

The Hanging-Cloud Bridge on Mount Gyodo, Ashikaga,
C. 1834.

"The Hanging-Cloud Bridge" on Mount Gyodo, Ashikaga,
C. 1834.

At Sea Off Kazusa

Taken from the series *Thirty-Six Views of Mount Fuji*.
C. 1830-1832, woodblock print.
26 × 38.4 cm.

Most of this composition is taken up by a large Chinese sailing ship, known as a junk, closely followed by another which is partly hidden from view. They are both depicted on a horizon shaped like a half-moon, making it look as if they are hanging in the air rather than floating on water. This effect is heightened by the use of similar shades of blue for both the sea and the sky. An opening in the hull reveals some human figures looking out to observe the scenery – or, more specifically, Mount Fuji, which is recognizable from afar. In fact it is the only identifiable element in this print, and as such brings a comforting touch to an otherwise bleak expanse of sea. The hoisted sails suggest that these boats are out on the open sea, while the turbulence of the water is conveyed by jerky black lines.

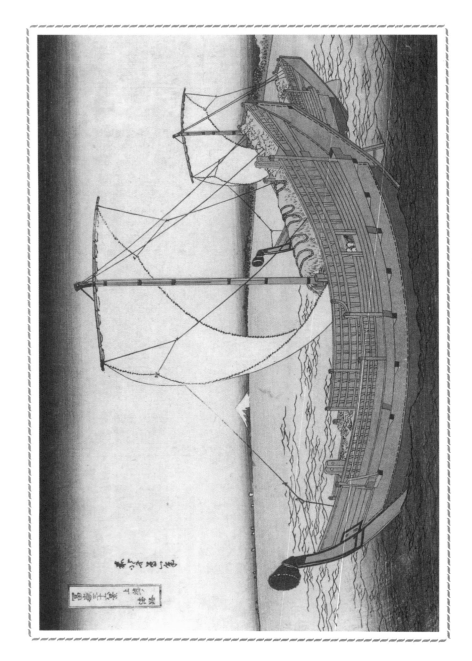

At Sea Off Kazusa, C. 1830-1832.

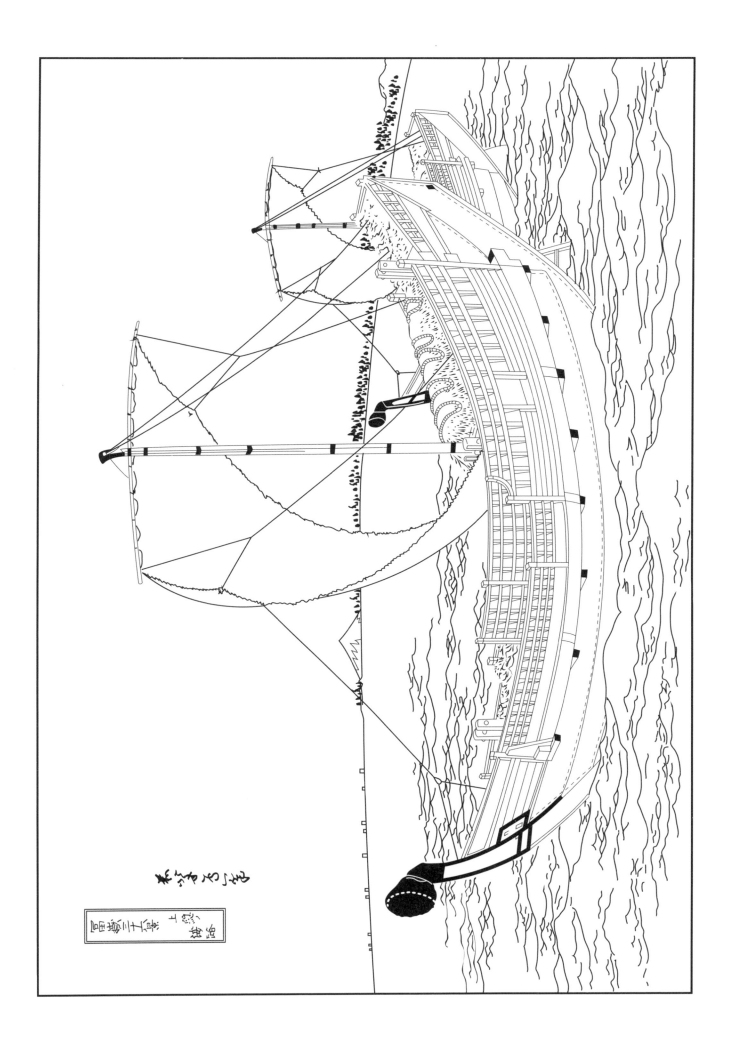

The Poet Fujiwara no Yoshitaka

Taken from the series *One Hundred Poems by One Hundred Poets*

Explained by a Wet Nurse.
C. 1835-1836, woodblock print.
24 × 35.6 cm.

Fujiwara no Yoshitaka was a famous Japanese poet and courtier who was renowned for his stylish elegance. The story goes that this famously handsome man preferred to commit suicide rather than endure the scars left on his face at the age of twenty by smallpox. Hokusai illustrated one of his poems in the series *One Hundred Poems by One Hundred Poets Explained by a Wet Nurse*. The subject is the poet's devotion to his beloved, who has turned his life upside down. Two men are bathing in the thermal pool, while on the terrace some people admire the stillness of the lake, which is set off by the steam emanating from the baths.

The Poet Fujiwara no Yoshitaka, C. 1835-1836.

The Poet Fujiwara no Yoshitaka, C. 1835-1836.

Kusunuki Tanmonmaru Masashige and Tsunehisa Betto of Yao

Taken from the series *Heroes in Combat*.
C. 1833-1834, woodblock print.
36.8 × 24.4 cm.

Our final drawing marks Hokusai's last return to military subjects, which he had abandoned for a time due to a brief foray into erotic prints. Masashige, at the top of the composition, is seen here battling with the warrior Tsunehisa by trying to knock him out with a block of stone bearing a truncated inscription. The characters' stiff expressions once again echo the theatrical poses that were so dear to Hokusai.

Graphically speaking, the composition is very dense, with various motifs superimposed onto each other. This accumulation of effects creates a confusion that is disorientating to the eye, thereby heightening the visceral impact of physical combat.

Kusunuki Tanmonmaru Masashige and Tsunehisa Betto of Yao,
C. 1833-1834.